Beginning Maps and

Maps are made by people to show where places are located. Maps help people find their way from one place to another.

In ancient times, people would draw simple maps in dirt or clay to show the way to a water hole or where food could be found.

Hundreds of years ago sailors, traders, and explorers made maps. These maps were not always accurate. But the more people explored the earth, the better the maps became.

You can learn how to read maps and globes. You can learn how to make maps.

Globes

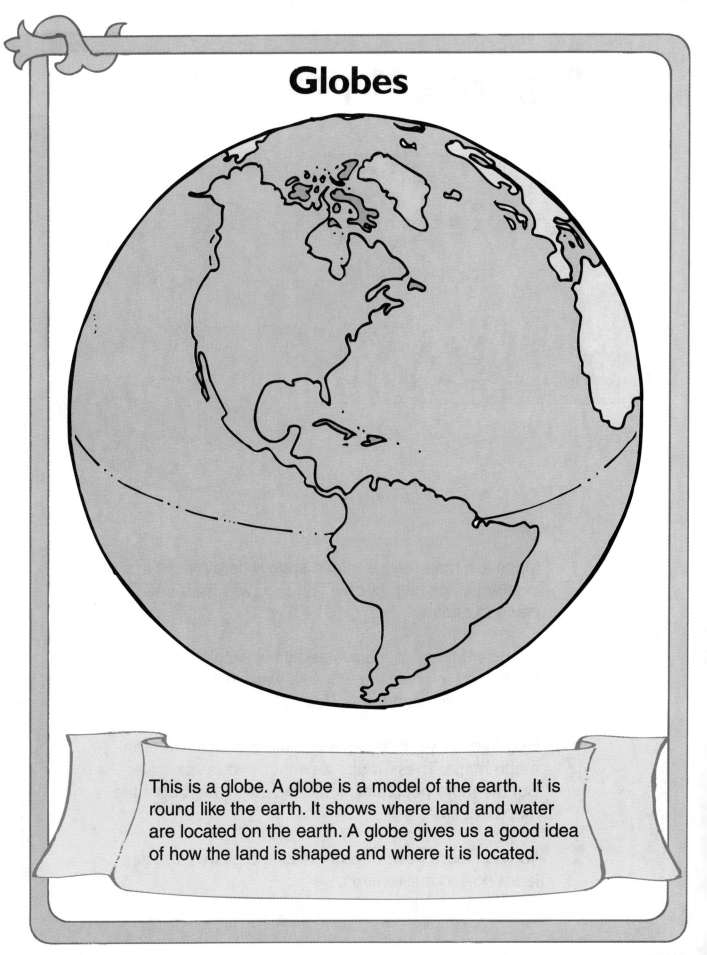

This is a globe. A globe is a model of the earth. It is round like the earth. It shows where land and water are located on the earth. A globe gives us a good idea of how the land is shaped and where it is located.

EMC 4134

Maps

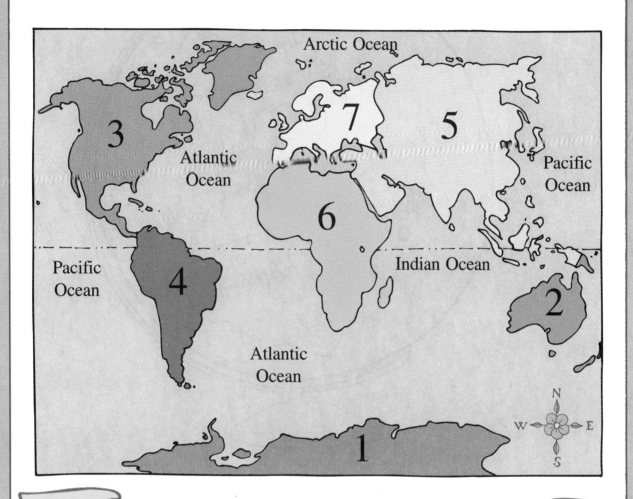

This is a map. A map is a flat picture of the earth. Maps show the land and water areas on the earth. But flat maps do not show the size and placement of land as well as they are shown on a globe.

The earth is divided into large land areas. These areas are called continents. There are 7 continents.

1. Antarctica
2. Australia
3. North America
4. South America
5. Asia
6. Africa
7. Europe

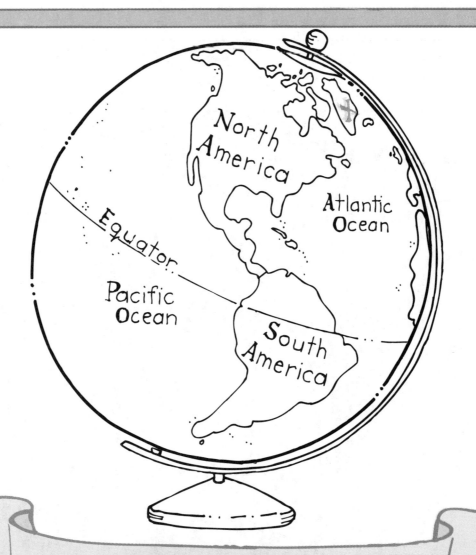

Using a Globe

This globe shows North America and South America.
Look at the shapes of the continents.

Find the big X. This is Greenland. Compare its size
and shape to Greenland on the map on page 5.

Color North America orange.
Color South America green.
Color the water blue.

If you live in North America make a red X on it.
If you live in South America make a blue X on it.

EMC 4134

Using a Map

This map shows North and South America too. Look at the shapes of the continents. Are they the same as they are on the globe on page 4?

Find the big X on Greenland. See how much bigger it looks on a map than on a globe.

Color North America orange.
Color South America green.
Color the water blue.

Making a Map

This is a picture of a backyard.

This is a map of the same backyard.
Each thing in the picture is shown by a symbol.
A symbol is a simple way of showing a real thing.

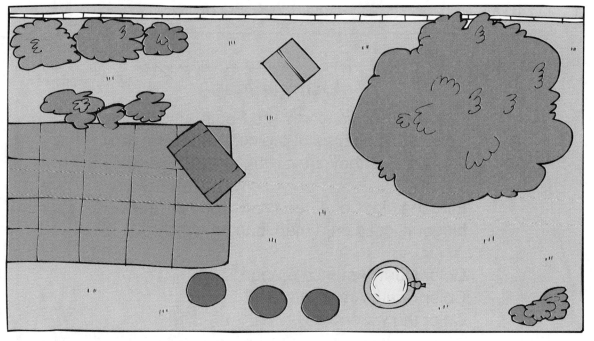

6

My Backyard

Make a map of your backyard.

Directions on a Map

North

West   East

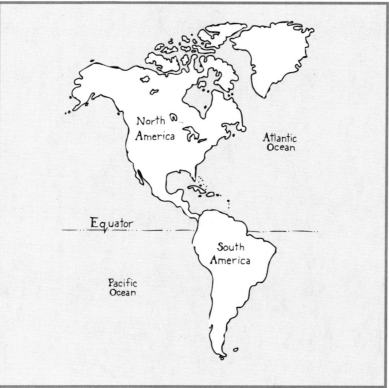

South

There are four basic directions on a map. These are north, south, east, and west. The directions help you locate places on a map.

Some maps have the words north, south, east, and west printed on the sides of the map.

Most maps show the directions in a compass rose. The compass rose is set on the page so that the "N" is pointing north.

EMC 4134

Where Is It?

north   south   east   west

Write the four directions in the correct places on this map.

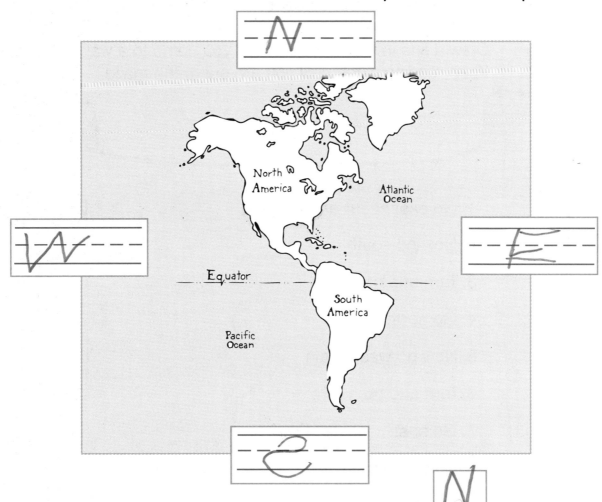

N

W

E

S

North America

Atlantic Ocean

Equator

South America

Pacific Ocean

Write N, S, E, W in the correct places to show north, south, east, and west on this compass rose.

N

W

E

S

Using a Compass Rose

Use the compass rose to help you find
your way out of the maze on page 11.

Start at the **X** in the center of the maze.
Read a clue to see which way to go.
Draw a line in that direction until you come to a wall.
Keep reading clues until you are out of the maze.

1. Go east as far as you can.

2. Now go south.

3. Turn and go west.

4. Go north.

5. Now go west again.

6. Turn and go north.

7. Go east.

8. Now go north.

9. Go east again.

10. Turn and go south.

11. Go east for the last time.

12. Now go north.

Hurray! You made it!

EMC 4134

Find Your Way Out of the Maze

Can you find any other ways to get out of the maze?
Start at the X. Follow the arrow.

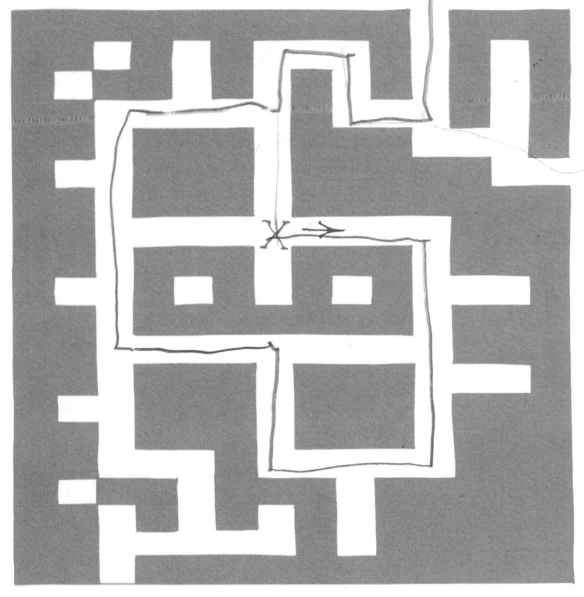

Around the Park

Color the pictures on the map on page 13 to answer these questions.

1. What is east of the water fountain?
   Color it brown.

2. What is west of the slide?
   Color it red.

3. What is just north of the tether ball?
   Color it blue.

4. What is south of the picnic table?
   Color it orange.

5. What is just west of the climbing bars?
   Color it yellow and brown.

6. Draw yourself north of the sandbox.

EMC 4134

Park Map

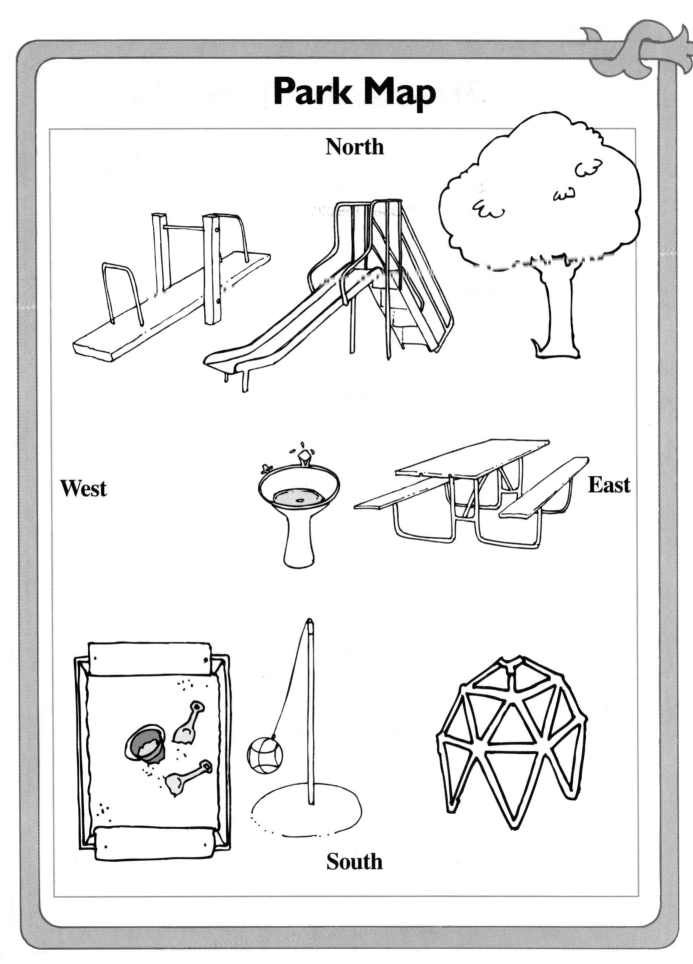

North

West

East

South

Find the Hidden Treasure

Follow these steps on the map on page 15 to find the treasure. Draw a line to show where you go.

1. Start at the cabin.
   Take water and a snack.

2. Go north until you get to the woods.
   Rest under a tree if you are tired.

3. Go west until you reach the cave.
   Sh! Don't wake the bear.

4. Go south until you get to the river.
   Walk across the log. Don't fall in!

5. Go east. Walk behind the hills.

6. Turn and walk south until you get to three large rocks.

7. Dig under the rock on the west side.

Hurray! You found the treasure.

EMC 4134

Treasure Map

Hemispheres

There is an imaginary line that goes around the middle of the Earth. It is the **Equator**. The Equator divides Earth in half. Each half is called a **hemisphere**.

All the land above the Equator is in the **northern hemisphere**.
All the land below the Equator is in the **southern hemisphere**.

Do you live in the northern hemisphere or in the southern hemisphere? _____

Some countries along the equator are in both hemispheres. Where is the country in which you live?

_____ My country is in the northern hemisphere.

_____ My country is in the southern hemisphere.

_____ My country is in both hemispheres.

EMC 4134

Lines on a Map and Globe

The Equator is not the only line on a map or globe. There are other imaginary lines that help people find places.

Some of these lines go in the same direction as the Equator. These lines are called **latitude**. They tell how far north or south you are. You count from the zero lino. It is the Equator.

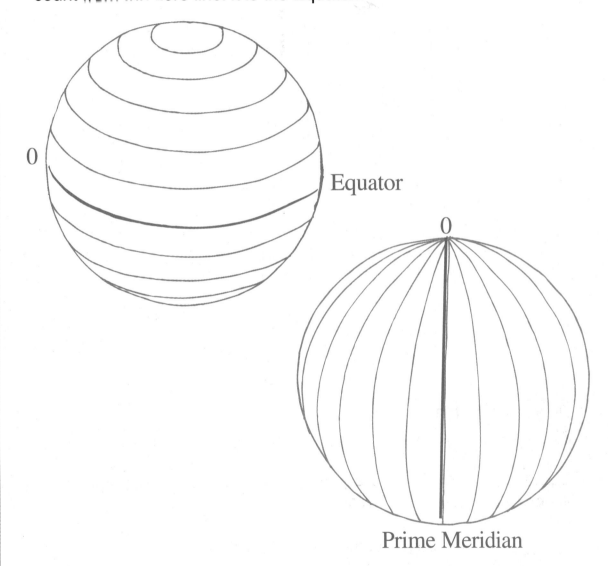

0

Equator

0

Prime Meridian

Some of these lines go from the north pole to the south pole. These lines are called **longitude**. They tell how far west or east you are. You count from the zero line. It is called the **Prime Meridian.**

Finding Places on a Map

You can use the number on each line of latitude and longitude to find the location of any place on Earth.

Start counting at the circle in the middle of the "map" where the zero lines cross.

Start at the circle in the middle.
Go west to 20.
Now go north to 20.
Did you get to the star?

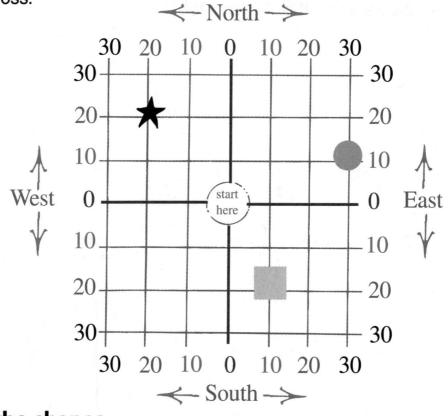

Find the shapes.

1. Start at the circle. Go 30 east.
   Now go 10 north.
   What shape did you find?

2. Start at the circle. Go 10 east.
   Now go 20 south.
   What shape did you find?

Using Longitude and Latitude

Find the pictures.
Color them.

red - 10 west and 20 south   purple - east 10 and 10 south
green - 20 east and 20 north   yellow - west 40 and 10 south
blue - 40 west and 30 north   black - west 30

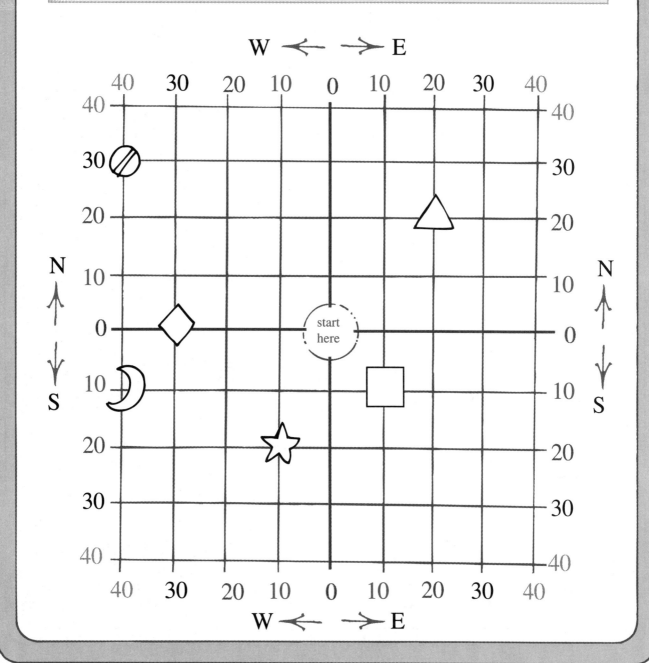

Map Legend

A map legend shows symbols for information on the map.
The legend is usually in a box near the bottom of the map.

This legend shows land forms.   **This legend shows man-made objects.**

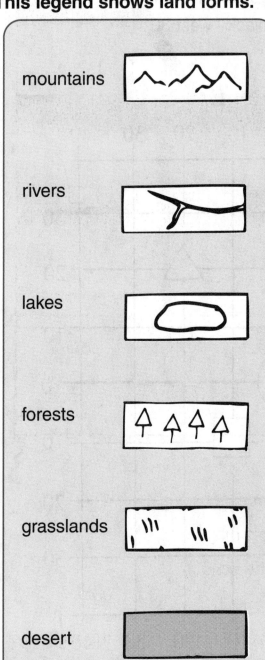

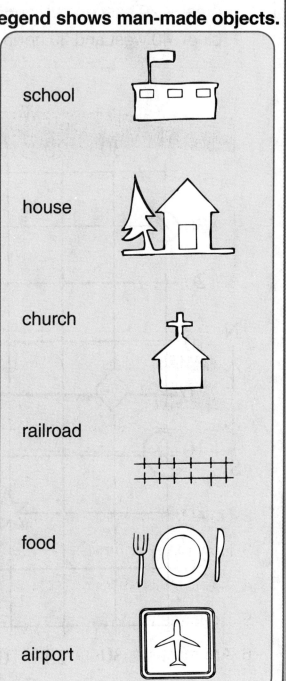

20

Using a Legend

Use the legend on this map to help you answer the questions below.

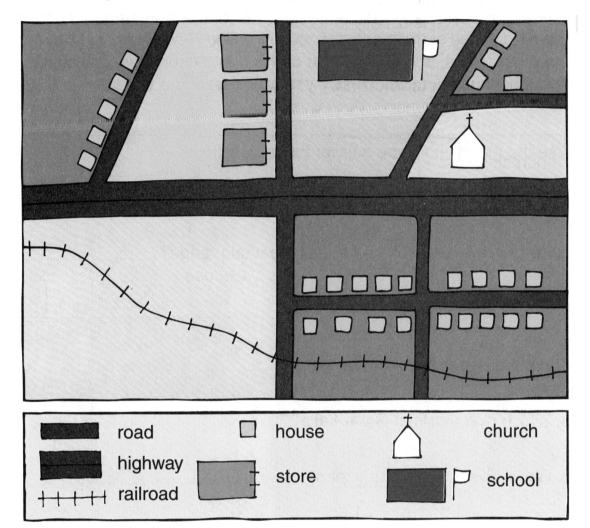

road   house   church

highway

store   school

railroad

1. Is the school north or south of the highway?_____

2. Does the railroad run north-south or does it run east-west? _____

3. How many churches do you find on this map? _____

4. Are the stores found east or west of the school? _____

5. Does the highway run from north to south? _____

6. Are more houses found north of the highway or south of the highway?

_____

Physical Maps

There are many kinds of maps. Each kind shows different information.

A physical map shows the natural features of the land. Page 23 contains a physical map of an imaginary country called Newlandia. You can find the rivers, lakes, and oceans. You can find the mountains, grasslands, and a desert. If you look closely you can even find a volcano.

Use the map to help you answer these questions:

1. What is the name of the longest river? _____

2. What is the name of the longest mountain range? _____

3. What is the name of the volcano? _____

4. What is the name of the desert? _____

5. Which river starts at Great Lake? _____

6. Which rivers end at the ocean? _____

   _____

7. Name the other bodies of water on the map.

   _____ Ocean   Strait of _____

   _____ Sea   Gulf of _____

   _____ Lake

EMC 4134

A Physical Map of Newlandia

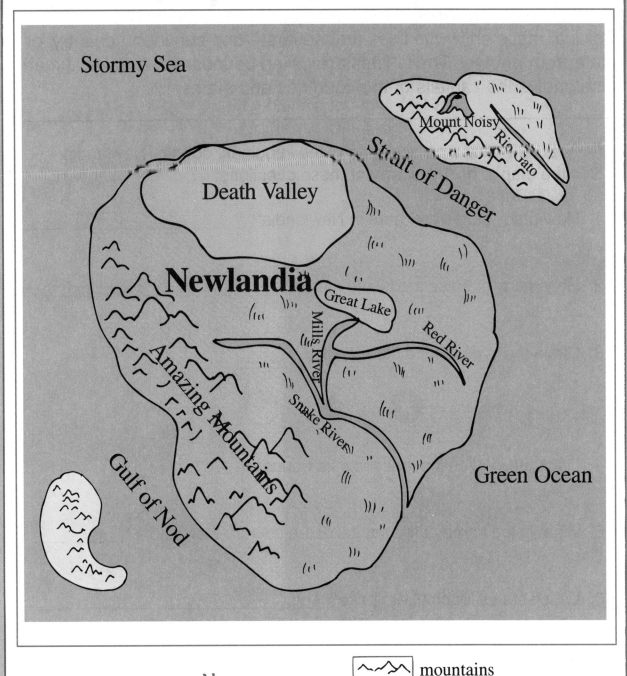

Stormy Sea

Mount Noisy

Rio Gato

Strait of Danger

Death Valley

Newlandia

Great Lake

Mills River

Red River

Snake River

Amazing Mountains

Gulf of Nod

Green Ocean

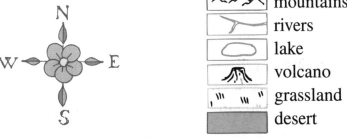

N
W — E
S

⌒⌒⌒ mountains
rivers
lake
volcano
grassland
desert

Political Maps

Political maps show the lines that separate one continent, country, or state from another. These lines are called boundaries. A political map also shows the capitals of the countries and states.

Page 25 contains a political map of the imaginary country Newlandia. Use the map to help you answer these questions:

1. How many states are there in Newlandia? _____

2. How many of these are island states? _____

3. Circle the symbol for a state capital.

   ★   ★   ○

4. Draw the kind of line that shows a boundary.

5. What is the name of the capital of the country Newlandia? _____

6. Which states touch Great Lake? _____

7. On which island is the capital city Tapa? _____

8. Which of these cities is the capital city of Bismark?

   Bayview   San Martin

A Political Map of Newlandia

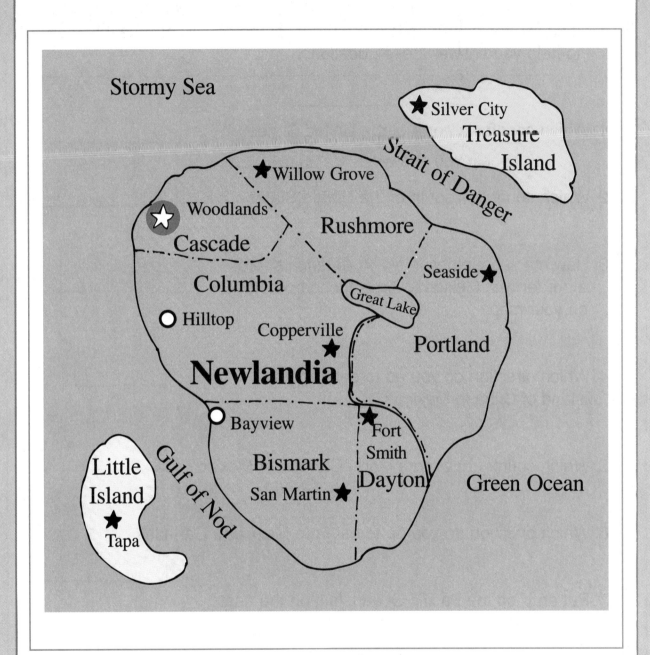

Stormy Sea

Silver City

Treasure Island

Strait of Danger

Willow Grove

Woodlands

Cascade

Rushmore

Columbia

Seaside

Great Lake

Hilltop

Copperville

Portland

Newlandia

Bayview

Little Island

Gulf of Nod

Bismark

San Martin

Fort Smith

Dayton

Green Ocean

Tapa

N
W E
S

Newlandia Political Map
Capital of Country
State Capitals
Other Cities
Boundaries
Rivers

EMC 4134

North America

Page 27 contains a political map of the continent of North America. It shows the countries that are a part of the continent. Use this map to help you answer these questions.

1. Which country is north of the United States? _____

2. Which country is south of the United States? _____

3. How many countries in North America share a border with Mexico? Circle these borders on your map. _____

4. Which direction do you go to get from the island of Cuba to Mexico? _____

5. Which country has more land - Canada or Mexico? _____

6. Which direction do you go to get from Mexico to Canada?

_____

7. Put an X on the Pacific Ocean. Is it on the east side or the west side of North America?

_____

8. Match these countries to their capital cities.

Mexico	Ottawa
United States	Mexico City
Canada	Washington, D.C.

EMC 4134

North America

Greenland

Canada

Pacific
Ocean

Ottawa

United States

Washington, D.C.

Atlantic
Ocean

Mexico

Cuba

Mexico City

Belize

Honduras

Guatemala

Nicaragua

El Salvador

Costa Rica

Panama

N
W   E
S

The Seven Continents
A Puzzle

Paste puzzle pieces here to make a map.

EMC 4134

Cut out the puzzle pieces.
Paste the pieces in place on page 28 and show a map of the seven continents.

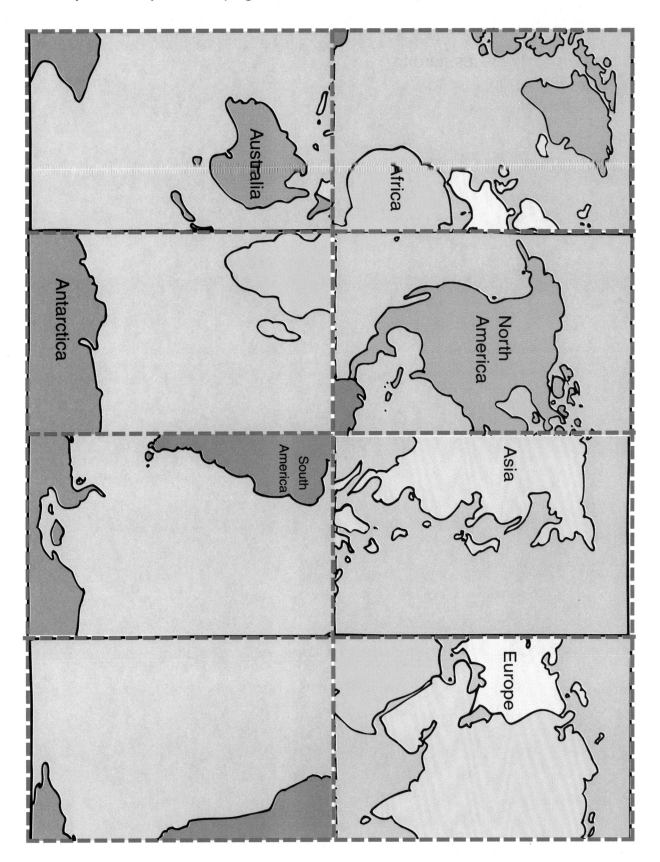

The Seven Continents

Write the name of each continent:

1. _____

2. _____

3. _____

4. _____

5. _____

6. _____

7. _____

Use the map on page 28.
Follow these directions:

1. Start at South America.

2. Draw a line east from South America to Africa.

3. Draw a line from Africa to North America.

4. Draw a line from North America to Europe.

5. Draw a line east from Europe to Asia.

6. Draw a line from Asia to Australia.

7. Now draw a line from Australia to Antarctica.

Hurray! You have visited all seven continents!

Answer Key

Please take time to go over the work your child has completed. Ask your child to explain what he/she has done. Praise both success and effort. If mistakes have been made, explain what the answer should have been and how to find it. Let your child know that mistakes are a part of learning. The time you spend with your child helps let him/her know you feel learning is important.

page 4

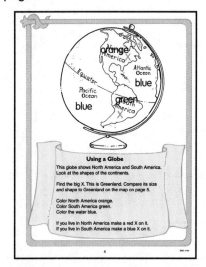

page 5

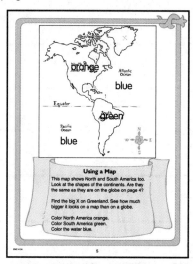

page 7

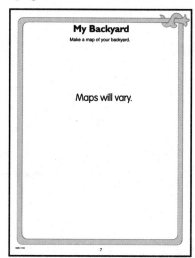

page 9

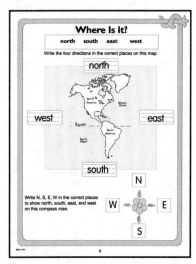

page 11

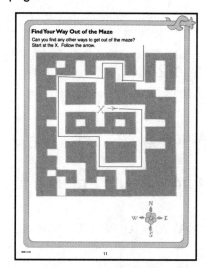

page 13

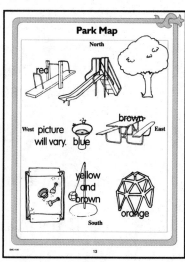

page 15

page 16

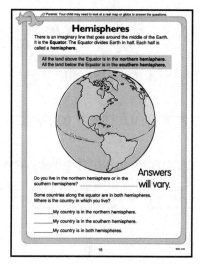

page 18

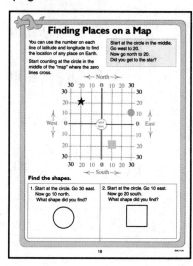